D0622916

Walker, Dal Jack London and Con
1st ed. Gaslight Publications,
3 3029 00862 6855

CENTRAL

OCT - 1982

SHERLOCK HOLMES
MONOGRAPH SERIES

Books by Dale L. Walker

The Lost Revolutionary: A Biography of John Reed (with Richard O'Connor), 1967.

The Fiction of Jack London: A Chronological Bibliography, 1972.

The Alien Worlds of Jack London, 1973.

Death Was the Black Horse: The Story of Rough Rider "Buckey" O'Neill, 1975.

Curious Fragments: Jack London's Tales of Fantasy Fiction, 1976.

No Mentor But Myself: Jack London, the Writer's Writer, 1979.

Only the Clouds Remain: Ted Parsons of the Lafayette Escadrille, 1980.

Jack London.

JACK LONDON
AND
CONAN DOYLE
A LITERARY KINSHIP

Dale L. Walker

ILLUSTRATED WITH PHOTOGRAPHS

GASLIGHT
PUBLICATIONS

BLOOMINGTON, INDIANA   1981

Copyright © 1970 by The Baker Street Irregulars

Copyright © 1974, 1981 by Dale L. Walker

All Rights Reserved

ISBN: 0-934468-03-6

Library of Congress
Catalogue Card No. 80-67698

First Edition: February 1981

Printed in the United States of America

GASLIGHT PUBLICATIONS
112 East Second
Bloomington, Indiana 47401

CENTRAL
C . 1

Dedication

To Alvin S. Fick

"I salute you . . . S. Holmes."
— Jack London, *Jerry of the Islands,* Chapter xx

"It's a very cheery thing to come into London by any of these lines."
— Sherlock Holmes in "The Naval Treaty"

"Who but Jack London would have written those words?"
— Sir Arthur Conan Doyle, *The Edge of the Unknown,*
Chapter vi

Contents

Sherlock Holmes and Dr. Watson, as depicted by Sidney Paget for the STRAND *magazine.*

Prologue

Holmes had been seated for some hours in silence with his long, thin back curved over a chemical vessel in which he was brewing a particularly malodorous product. His head was sunk upon his breast, and he looked from my point of view like a strange, lank bird, with dull gray plumage and a black top-knot.

"So, Watson," said he, suddenly, "you do not propose to invest in South African securities?"

I gave a start of astonishment. Accustomed as I was to Holmes's curious faculties, this sudden intrusion into my most intimate thoughts was utterly inexplicable.

"How on earth do you know that?" I asked.

He wheeled round upon his stool, with a steaming test-tube in his hand, and a gleam of amusement in his deep-set eyes.

"Now, Watson, confess yourself utterly taken aback," said he.
"I am."

"I ought to make you sign a paper to that effect."
"Why?"

"Because in five minutes you will say that it is all so absurdly simple."

"I am sure that I shall say nothing of the kind." . . .

"Here are the missing links of the very simple chain: 1. You had chalk between your left finger and thumb when you returned from the club last night. 2. You put chalk there when you play billiards, to steady the cue. 3. You never play billiards except with Thurston. 4. You told me, four weeks ago, that Thurston had an option on some South African property which would expire in a month, and which he desired you to share with him. 5. Your cheque book is locked in my drawer, and you have not asked for the key. 6. You do not propose to invest your money in this manner."

"How absurdly simple!" I cried.

— "The Dancing Men"

In the 1911 Jack London story, "A Goboto Night,"[1] one of a series of tales about the South Sea adventurer Captain David Grief, a character named Peter Gee, more than any other in London's vast corpus of fiction, demonstrates his creator's singular familiarity with the methods of Sherlock Holmes of Baker Street.

The scene takes place at the dinner table on Goboto Island, where a group of salt-seasoned men of the sea have gathered to exchange information on the state of the copra production and various blackbirding operations, as well as on the whereabouts of certain eminent seamen — in all, the sundry foc's'le scuttlebutt of a sailorish gathering.

Of the confraternity, two men stand out. One is the half-caste pearl buyer Peter Gee, whose exotic career has led him from Ceylon to the Paumotus; a man who, as London puts it, "had the stolid integrity of the Chinese blood that toned the recklessness and licentiousness of the English blood which had run in his father's veins." Gee is better educated than any man at table, speaking impeccable English and, when the occasion demands, showing a proficiency in several other tongues as well. He "knew and lived more of their own ideals of gentlemanness than they did themselves," London describes him, adding, "And finally, he was a gentle soul. Violence he deprecated, though he had killed men in his time. Turbulence he abhorred."[2]

The second principal figure in the scene is Alfred Deacon, an argumentative Australian with a propensity for truculence and caddishness that is exceeded only by his hyperdeveloped self-confidence.

As the pointless conversation hums on, the rumble of an anchor-chain through a hawsepipe is heard in the distance, tokening the arrival of a vessel offshore:

" 'It's David Grief,' Peter Gee remarked.

" 'How do you know?' Deacon demanded."

---

[1] *Saturday Evening Post,* September 30, 1911; included in the collection *A Son of the Sun.*

[2] Peter Gee appears in two other stories in *A Son of the Sun:* "The Feathers of the Sun" and "The Pearls of Parlay."

Gee's splendid deductive analysis that follows indelibly marks Jack London as a devotee of the unparalleled career of the world's greatest consulting detective. And, although considerable further evidence will be offered ("It is a capital mistake to theorize before you have all the evidence," Holmes warned in *A Study in Scarlet*), nothing is quite so conclusive as the quintessential Sherlockian monologue that follows Alfred Deacon's challenge:

"By the sound it was a small craft – no square-rigger. No whistle, no siren, was blown – again a small craft. It anchored close in – still again a small craft, for steamers and big ships must drop hook outside the middle shoal. Now the entrance is tortuous. There is no recruiting nor trading captain in the group who dares to run the passage after dark. Certainly no stranger would. There *were* two exceptions. The first was Margonville. But he was executed by the High Court at Fiji. Remains the other exception, David Grief. Night or day, in any weather, he runs the passage. This is well known to all. A possible factor, in case Grief were somewhere else, would be some young dare-devil of a skipper. In this connection, in the first place, I don't know of any, nor does anybody else. In the second place, David Grief is in these waters, cruising on the *Gunga,* which is shortly scheduled to leave here for Karo-Karo. I spoke to Grief, on the *Gunga,* in Sandfly Passage, day before yesterday. He was putting a trader ashore on a new station. He said he was going to call in at Babo, and then come on to Goboto. He has had ample time to get here. I have heard an anchor drop. Who else than David Grief can it be?"

To clinch the argument, Gee adds a Holmesian dramatic touch:

"In a few minutes David Grief will enter through that door and say, 'In Guvutu they merely drink between drinks.' I'll wager fifty pounds he's the man that enters and that his words will be 'In Guvutu they merely drink between drinks.' "

A few minutes later, Gee's scenario is enacted to the letter. As London wrote in a far different work: "Shades of Old Sleuth and Sherlock Holmes!"[3]

---

[3] *The People of the Abyss.* The expression is found in Chapter II. *Old Sleuth* was a lurid and popular detective magazine of the day.

Flora Wellman, the mother of Jack London.

1 Jack

JACK LONDON, described by his latest biographer as having "towered like a Colossus over his time,"[1] was born John Griffith Chaney on January 12, 1876, and the nature of his birth and youth would seem to have augered against his towering over anything.

He was the bastard son of William H. Chaney, an itinerant Maine-born writer, editor, and astrologer, and Flora Wellman of Massillon, Ohio, a neurotic spiritualist. Eight months after this strange pair parted company in San Francisco, where their son was born, Flora married a kind-hearted, dirt-poor farmer from Pennsylvania named John London, who gave the baby his name.[2]

The following chronology touches on the signal events of Jack London's life and career.

1892: On his sloop *Razzle-Dazzle,* became "Prince of the Oyster Pirates" on San Francisco Bay, poaching from privately-owned oyster beds; later served as a law enforcement officer of the Fish Patrol.

1893: Signed on before the mast of the sealing schooner *Sophia Sutherland,* sailing to Japan and the Bering Sea. In November, wrote an essay, "Story of a Typhoon Off the Coast of Japan," which won first prize in a San Francisco newspaper contest. It was an auspicious debut for a writer of seventeen. He described what it was like to be below decks on the schooner as the storm raged:

The wildly dancing movements of the sea lamp cast a pale flickering light through the fo'c'sle and turned to golden honey the drops of water on the yellow oilskins. In all the corners dark shadows seemed to come

---

[1] Andrew Sinclair, *Jack,* p. 248.

[2] See the bibliography for the chief London and Doyle bibliographies.

and go, while up in the eyes of her, beyond the pall bitts descending from deck to deck, where they seemed to lurk like some dragon in a cavern's mouth, it was dark as Erebus.[3]

1894: Joined the western detachment of "Coxey's Army" — the band of unemployed men organized by Ohioan Jacob S. Coxey in the depression following the Panic of 1893 — in its march to Washington, D.C., deserted in the midwest and rode the rails eastward. In Niagara Falls, New York, he was arrested for vagrancy and spent a month in the Erie County Penitentiary. Out of these experiences came a remarkable book, *The Road* (1907).

1895: Completed high school in Oakland, California; wrote sketches and stories for the student magazine, *Aegis.*

1896: Joined the Socialist Labor Party; attended the University of California at Berkeley for one semester.

1897: Joined the Klondike gold rush, a pivotal experience in his life, spending the winter on the Yukon and returning via a two-thousand-mile boat trip down the river. Arrived in Oakland with less than five ounces of gold in his possession but ready to mine the experience for a return any Argonaut would envy.

1899: Published his first "professional" story, "To the Man on the Trail," in the *Overland Monthly* and was paid $5 for it.[4]

1900: "An Odyssey of the North" published in *The Atlantic Monthly.* Married Bessie Maddern, and his first collection of stories, *The Son of the Wolf,* appeared.

1902: Traveled to London and lived for several weeks in the city's East End slum, gathering material for what became the sociological study *The People of the Abyss* (1903). His first major novel, a dismal failure titled *A Daughter of the Snows,* was published in October.

1903: *The Call of the Wild,* his most famous book, appeared.

---

[3] San Francisco *Morning Call,* November 12, 1893; reprinted in Irving Shepard (ed.), *Jack London's Tales of Adventure,* pp. 54–57.

[4] London's first commercial fiction sale had actually appeared in the New York magazine *Owl* in September 1897, but he forgot — or chose not to remember — the undistinguished "Two Gold Bricks" and always marked his debut as a professional writer with "To the Man on the Trail."

The young Jack London, at age 17, while serving on the SOPHIE SUTHERLAND *in 1897.*

1904: Sailed for Japan and Korea as war correspondent for the Hearst Syndicate in the Russo-Japanese War. *The Sea Wolf* published.

1905: Divorced Bessie Maddern and married Charmian Kittredge in Chicago. Began purchasing ranch property near Glen Ellen, north of San Francisco.

1906: Lectured at Yale. Reported on the San Francisco earthquake and fire. *White Fang,* a companion volume to *The Call of the Wild,* published.

1907-9: The voyage of the *Snark,* his private custom-made ketch, to Hawaii, the Marquesas, Tahiti, Samoa, Fiji, New Hebrides and Solomon Islands. *Martin Eden,* his great auto-biographical novel, published in September 1909.

1910: Added holdings to his "Beauty Ranch" near Glen Ellen.

1912: Sailed from Baltimore around Cape Horn aboard the four-masted barque *Dirigo.*

1913: Wolf House, his great four-storied mansion, mysteriously destroyed by fire before it could be occupied—a $70,000 loss. *John Barleycorn* published: a memorable semi-autobiographical treatise on alcoholism.

1914: Became correspondent for *Collier's* at $1100 a week in the Mexican Revolution.

1915: Revisited Hawaii to recuperate from health problems. Published his last great work, the novel *The Star Rover.*

1916: Resigned from the Socialist Party "because of its lack of fire and fight, and its loss of emphasis on the class struggle."[5]

Jack London died at 7:45 P.M., November 22, 1916, of uremic poisoning.

In a writing career of but eighteen years (1899-1916), he produced a prodigious 190 short stories, 22 novels, something over 450 non-fiction works—essays, reviews, newspaper stories—plus several plays and poems. The best of this work is represented in his 53 books, translated into over 40 languages. His work is perenially popular in Europe—for many years he has been the most popular American author in the Soviet Union (where Sir Arthur Conan Doyle is said to be the most popular

---

[5]King Hendricks and Irving Shepard (eds.), *Letters from Jack London,* p. 467.

British writer)—and a resurgence of interest in him occurred throughout the 1970s and shows no sign of abating.

"I've had no mentor but myself," he wrote his editor at Houghton Mifflin on the eve of publication of his first book in 1900,[6] and he was as furiously self-educated as he was a liver and lover of life.

The wolf was his personal symbol. His first book bore the word in its title, and one of his greatest fictional creations was Wolf Larsen of *The Sea Wolf*; he signed letters to intimates "Wolf," his bookplate depicted a wolf's head, his baronial home in the Valley of the Moon was "Wolf House"—and the ruins of it are still so named.

---

[6] *Ibid.*, p. 87.

"Johnny" London, aged 9 or 10, shortly before moving with his mother and adoptive father to Oakland, California from their Livermore Valley farm.

2 In the Abyss

IN the spring of 1886, when Dr. A. Conan Doyle of Bush Villas, Southsea, was putting the final touches on the manuscript of *A Study in Scarlet,* which would introduce Sherlock Holmes, John H. Watson, M.D., and 221B Baker Street to the world, Jack London was ten years old and with his family had just moved back to Oakland after gamely trying to scratch a living from the soil of Livermore Valley. Jack — or Johnny, as he was then called — was attending Garfield School in Oakland and had made one of the most important discoveries of his life: the city's public library.[1]

While London probably discovered Sherlock Holmes at an early age, it is of course improbable that *A Study in Scarlet,* in either of its first two English editions — the 1887 *Beeton's Christmas Annual* or the 1888 Ward, Lock & Co. volume — could have been found in the Oakland Public Library. Perhaps the first American edition, that published by J. B. Lippincott Co. in 1890, was there.

He was an omnivorous reader at an early age. While surviving on the Livermore farm, he had discovered such books as Horatio Alger's biography of James A. Garfield, *From Canal Boy to President* (1881), Washington Irving's *Alhambra* (1832), Paul du Chaillu's *Expeditions and Adventures in Equatorial Africa* (1861),[2] Ouida's *Signa* (1875), and Wilkie Collins's *The New Magdalen* (1873). At the Oakland library, his reading was given direction by Miss Ina Coolbrith, a poet laureate of California who had been one of the "Golden Gate Trinity" of

---

[1] Charmian K. London, *The Book of Jack London,* I, pp. 45–61.

[2] London frequently mentioned Du Chaillu's "African Travels," but the book was probably *Explorations and Adventures in Equatorial Africa.* The intrepid Du Chaillu (1835–1903) was an inspirational figure in London's formative years.

writers, with Bret Harte and Charles Warren Stoddard, on the *Overland Monthly.*

Miss Coolbrith (1845–1928) was a descendent of Joseph Smith, founder of the Church of Jesus Christ of Latter-Day Saints. It seems likely that she had considerable interest in "The Country of the Saints," the Utah chapters of *A Study in Scarlet.* This portion of the novel is sometimes compared to Bret Harte's style, and Doyle biographer Pierre Nordon says, "Bret Harte and Poe were his models."[3]

Interestingly, both Doyle and London wrote anti-Mormon works, or at least works in which the Mormons were villains. The Utah chapters of *A Study in Scarlet* are in the same school as the Mountain Meadows Massacre chapter of London's *The Star Rover* (1915), except that London's episode is tenaciously factual throughout, including such details as the surname, Fancher, of the young boy around whom the narrative is built, and the name and description of John D. Lee, the leader of the "Sons of Dan" who engineered the Fancher train massacre in 1857. On the other hand, as Jack Tracy's book-length treatment of the subject concludes, "The weight of literary evidence still would seem to indicate that the Mormon interlude of *A Study in Scarlet* is entirely fictitious."[4]

"I read everything," London wrote in his autobiographical work *John Barleycorn* (1913),

but principally history and adventure and all the old travels and voyages. I read mornings, afternoons and nights. I read in bed, I read at table, I read as I walked to and from school, and I read at recess while the other boys were playing.[5]

With such an appetite for history and adventure, it is possible that he also read such works as *Micah Clarke* (1889) and *The White Company* (1891) — works by Conan Doyle.

---

[3] Pierre Nordon, *Conan Doyle,* p. 78.

[4] Jack Tracy, *Conan Doyle and the Latter-Day Saints,* p. 67.

[5] *John Barleycorn,* p. 41.

Jack London's first serious examination of the Sherlock Holmes stories probably occurred in the period between 1899 and 1902. The latter date is beyond question, since it is the year London wrote *The People of the Abyss,* containing his first printed reference to Holmes. The earlier date marks London's first professionally-published work, and it was a period when the young writer was making a thorough study of the magazine "markets," trying to learn the secret "formula" by which other writers' stories were published while his own were being rejected with maddening regularity. In later years, writing autobiographically of these frustrating times, London reminisced:

My light burned till two and three in the morning, which led a good neighbor woman into a fit of sentimental Sherlock Holmes deduction. Never seeing me in the daytime, she concluded that I was a gambler, and that the light in my window was placed there by my mother to guide her erring son home.[6]

Perhaps his attention was drawn to back issues of *Harper's* magazine or *McClure's,* which, in 1893, ran *The Memoirs of Sherlock Holmes.* Both magazines were to become important publishers of London's work after 1900. And he surely knew of William Gillette's famed stage production of *Sherlock Holmes,* first launched at the Garrick Theatre in New York in 1899 and running for 230 performances before going on the road.

Certainly by the time of his return from Europe at the end of 1902, the manuscript of *The People of the Abyss* in his luggage, London was fully conscious of Conan Doyle, Doyle's fame and most famed literary creation.

It is fascinating to think of the common interests, other than their literary careers, that made kinsmen of the two men, despite the sad fact that they never met.

Doyle, when he was twenty-one, spent seven months at sea in 1880, in Greenland and Spitzbergen waters, on the 600-ton Peterhead steam whaler *Hope.* For the voyage he earned £50 as ship's surgeon and related his experiences on the *Hope* in the January 1897 issue of the *Strand* magazine. In 1881, he again

---

[6]*Ibid.,* p. 250.

went to sea, signing on the *Mayumba* to the Gold Coast of West Africa and enduring such experiences as contracting typhoid fever in Lagos, Nigeria, and coming close to being killed by a shark while swimming off the side of his ship.[7]

London, a lifelong sailor, had his first deepwater experience in 1893, aboard the three-topmast schooner *Sophia Sutherland,* on a sealing expedition to Japan and the North Pacific. He related some of his experiences on the voyage in the San Francisco *Morning Call* of November 12, 1893. His seaman's pay is not known, but he earned $25 for the newspaper article and the high-school dropout's satisfaction of winning first prize in a contest entered by students at Stanford and the University of California.

Another common ground was the Anglo-Boer War of 1899–1902. Doyle had volunteered for service in South Africa on Christmas Eve, 1899, and by April of the following year was in Bloemfontein, capital of the Orange Free State, working to put down an enteric fever epidemic. His 60,000-word, sixpence pamphlet, *The War in South Africa: Its Cause and Conduct* (1902), sold 300,000 copies in six weeks and another 50,000 in America and Canada.[8] It is a virtual certainty that Jack London, boning up on the war, read it.

London was sent to England by the American Press Association in the summer of 1902 to report on the aftermath of the war, which had ended the previous May 31 with the Treaty of Vereeniging. Upon arriving in the British capital in early August, a cable informed him that the APA had cancelled the assignment. Left in England with a return ticket and some cash, London spent seven weeks in the East End ghetto of the English metropolis, disguised appropriately as a seaman. His observations—a highly sensitive documentary—form his book, *The People of the Abyss.*

From Trafalgar Square, he saw the coronation procession of King Edward VII on August 9, 1902, a gorgeous imperial panoply of gold and glitter, splendid horsemen and carriages, uniforms and medals, the array of Pax Britannica on the march.

---

[7] Charles Higham, *The Adventures of Conan Doyle,* pp. 50–53.

[8] John Dickson Carr, *The Life of Sir Arthur Conan Doyle,* pp. 232–33.

Arthur Conan Doyle in 1892, at the beginning of the phenomenal success of Sherlock Holmes.

He stood with the ragged, hungry and hopeless denizens of the East End, and the contrast between them and the "vanity, show, and mumbo-jumbo foolery"[9] that passed by in the solemn rolling of drums, chink of sabre and spur, struck him as grotesque.

He spent his time with the worst East London had to offer, and in seven weeks finished his book. When it was published by Macmillan in October 1903, it shocked some readers and reviewers with its graphic eyewitness reportage. One quoted passage will suffice as a demonstration of what was considered, in 1903, as brutal writing. In company with two laborers, he walked along Mile End Road in the heart of the East End, and told of his companions keeping their eyes glued on the pavement and of their stopping frequently to pick things up from the street. Cigar and cigarette butts, he thought at first, but no:

From the slimy sidewalk, they were picking up bits of orange peel, apple skin, and grape stems, and they were eating them. The pits of green gage plums they cracked between their teeth for the kernels inside. They picked up stray crumbs of bread the size of peas, apple cores so black and dirty one would not take them to be apple cores, and these things these two men took into their mouths and chewed them, and swallowed them; and this between six and seven o'clock in the evening of August 20, year of our Lord 1902, in the heart of the greatest, wealthiest, and most powerful empire the world has ever seen.[10]

He said that the East End was called "The City of Dreadful Monotony" by some, especially the "well-fed, optimistic sight-seers who look over the surface of things and are merely shocked by the intolerable sameness and meanness of it all," but, he added:

If the East End is worthy of no worse title than the City of Dreadful Monotony, and if working people are unworthy of variety and beauty and surprise, it would not be such a bad place in which to live. But the East End does merit a worse title. It should be called The City of Degradation.[11]

---

[9] *The People of the Abyss,* p. 146.   [10] *Ibid.,* p. 78.   [11] *Ibid.,* p. 211.

"Tottery old men and women were searching in the garbage thrown in the mud." One of the many illustrations accompanying THE PEOPLE OF THE ABYSS.

The book had mixed reviews. Some critics thought it deserved to stand beside Jacob Riis's *How the Other Half Lives* (1890) as an indictment of poverty-amongst-riches mismanagement. A modern London biographer and an Englishman, Robert Barltrop, has researched the reaction in his country to the book and says: "English critics were favourably impressed and agreed that Jack London had come closer to the heart of the East End slums than any other writer."[12] But the *Nation* commented caustically that London "describes the East End as Dante might have described the Inferno, had he been a yellow journalist," the *Atlantic Monthly* said the book was "deficient in the firmness and dignity of mood and touch which might have made it literature," and the *Bookman* accused London of "snobbishness because of his profound consciousness of the gulf fixed between the poor denizens of the Abyss and the favoured class of which he is the proud representative."[13] London must have smiled over that last incredible phrase.

To this day, there is division of opinion on it. Seventy-five years after publication of *The People of the Abyss,* the book apparently still retains the power to enrage. Andrew Sinclair, an Englishman and a biographer of Dylan Thomas, in his 1977 biography of Jack London, says repeatedly that London went to the East End with his mind made up on what he would find there:

As an evolutionary Socialist, he had already preconceived his vision of the East End as the Black Hole of capitalism, the slough of human hope.[14]

But given the overwhelming evidence of the nature of East London when *The People of the Abyss* was being written, in which hunting for poverty there would be like hunting for pus in an abcess, Sinclair's overwrought point of view is ridiculous. A more balanced opinion is that of the other modern English biographer of London, Robert Barltrop:

---

[12] Robert Barltrop, *Jack London: The Man, the Writer, the Rebel,* p. 52.

[13] Philip Foner, *Jack London: American Rebel,* p. 52.

[14] Sinclair, p. 87.

It is not a propaganda work except in the sense that to draw attention to an evil can in itself provoke the demand for change. . . . To anyone who reads it, it is a trenchant and compelling account of the slums of London.[15]

Although London missed any part of the South African campaign itself, he had strong feelings that "the Boers are anachronisms,"[16] and his sympathy for England's position in the war would have endeared him to Arthur Conan Doyle — now Sir Arthur, knighted by King Edward VII on Coronation Day, August 9 past.

There is yet a third area of kinship between London and Doyle, the spiritualist link, and while it would have been a more one-sided affair, each would have benefited from the other's experiences in it. Sir Arthur had his first experience with the paranormal in 1879, had joined the Society for Psychical Research in 1893, and by 1915 was a staunch believer in spiritualism. Jack London was born into it.

---

[15] Barltrop, p. 188.

[16] Hendricks and Shepard, p. 66.

Sir Arthur Conan Doyle in later life, once he had embarked upon his spiritualist quest.

3 The Spiritualistic Link

LONDON'S MOTHER, Flora Wellman, was an ardent spiritualist, and her common-law husband, "Professor" William Henry Chaney, London's putative father, was by all accounts a serious astrologer and dabbler in the occult. At the time of Conan Doyle's all-out conversion to true believer, however, Jack London was writing: "I was born amongst spiritualists and lived my childhood and boyhood life amongst spiritualists. The result of this close contact was to make an unbeliever out of me."[1]

Such an attitude would not have daunted Doyle but would have interested him greatly. Holmes's creator doubtlessly knew that, despite the disclaimer, the American author had a decided proclivity toward that parapsychological gray area, the "unknown." London experimented in his fiction with a variety of occult plots, from as early as 1895 to his last days. He wrote of ghosts, death and rejuvenation, the mysteries of the Ouija board, invisibility, revenge from the grave, transmigration, reincarnation, dystopic futures, and atavistic dreams.[2]

Two of London's novels in particular show this aspect of the London-Doyle kinship. In *The Star Rover*,[3] the overlapping themes are the horrors and dehumanization of prison life, transmigration, and reincarnation—all subjects of intense interest to Conan Doyle.

And when, in Chapter 5 of *A Study in Scarlet,* Holmes remarks to Watson, "There are vague memories in our souls of

---

[1] Hendricks and Shepard, p. 444.

[2] See Dale L. Walker, *The Alien Worlds of Jack London* and *Curious Fragments: Jack London's Tales of Fantasy Fiction.*

[3] Serialized in the Los Angeles *Examiner American Sunday Monthly Magazine,* February 14–October 10, 1914.

those misty centuries when the world was in its childhood," one can almost visualize Jack London's reaction. Holmes's observation is an *exact* description of the theme of one of London's best-loved works, *Before Adam*.[4] Says the narrator in this story:

> "I have visions of myself roaming through the forests of the Younger World, and yet it is not myself that I see but one that is only remotely a part of me, as my father and my grandfather are parts of me less remote. This other-self of mine is an ancestor, a progenitor of my progenitors in the early line of my race, himself the progeny of a line that long before his time developed fingers and toes and climbed up into the trees."[5]

While London could not be credited with being the first writer to adapt Darwinism to fiction, his contribution in *Before Adam* is considerable. A novelette of atavistic dreams, *Before Adam* takes a young man of modern times back to pre-history, where, as a member of a tribe known as "the Folk," he becomes "Big-Tooth." The story, synoptic in nature with no beginning or end, concerns the tribe's attempts to adapt to life on the ground after centuries of life in the trees. London's Big-Tooth is a man of the Paleolithic age, and the novel carries the theme of the overlapping of the Paleo- and Neolithic ages, racial memory, and the idea that in man's mind are preserved old fears and passions of his Stone Age ancestry.

In his last book, *The Edge of the Unknown* (1930), Conan Doyle devotes considerable space to a purported spiritual encounter that Edward Biron Payne claimed to have had with the deceased Jack London. Payne's relationship, and that of Payne's wife, with London — information clearly unknown to Sir Arthur — is worth examining at this point, before recounting the strange episode subscribed to so strongly by the creator of Sherlock Holmes.

---

[4] Serialized in *Everybody's Magazine,* October 1906–February 1907.

[5] *Before Adam,* p. 19.

Payne, a former Congregational Church minister, "became convert to certain non-sectarian doctrines"[6] and worked in the Unitarian Church movement for a number of years before retiring from religious life. In 1899, he became an editor on the *Overland Monthly* and thus became familiar, at the earliest stage, with Jack London's literary career.

In 1910, Payne married Ninetta Eames, aunt of London's second wife Charmian Kittredge, thus strengthening his relationship with the now world-famous author. Ten years earlier, Ninetta, then wife of Roscoe Eames, business manager on the *Overland* and later the self-proclaimed but ludicrously inept skipper of London's *Snark,* had effected the first meeting between London and Charmian. Moreover, Ninetta Eames had been among the first to write *about* Jack London. In an article in the *Overland* in 1900, she wrote that his fiction derived from a childhood "cramped and embittered by omnipresent poverty," years of reading, adventures as a sailor, a "secular evangelist for Socialism," a tramp and Klondike gold-seeker. She said his writing combined fact, fantasy, "frank and wholesome sentiment," and that these, "with his assiduous application, his indomitable purpose...gave promise and prophecy of exceptional achievement."[7]

Small wonder, in those early days, that London called Ninetta "Mother Mine."

But by the time Edward Payne married her, London's warmth toward Ninetta and considerably subsided. He had made a drastic mistake in having her serve as his business manager in 1907-9, when he and Charmian sailed the South Seas on the *Snark*. Mrs. Eames had made a hideous botch of his affairs and was relieved of her duties when London returned home.[8]

---

[6] Edward B. Payne, *The Soul of Jack London,* p. viii. The Kingsport, Tenn. printing quoted is the second edition of the book, containing a preface by Ninetta Eames Payne. The first edition was published in London in 1926.

[7] Ninetta Eames, "Jack London," *Overland Monthly,* May 1900, pp. 417-25.

[8] Sinclair, p. 159.

It was typical of the great-hearted and forgiving Jack that he gave Ninetta and her new husband an expensive wedding gift, but he thereafter evinced little affection toward either of them.

Just two weeks before London's death, in November 1916, Ninetta and Edward Payne entered London's life for the last time. (As will be seen, they would enter his death a few years hence.) The Paynes, together with some other Glen Ellen residents, sued London in a water rights dispute. The case came to court on November 8, lasted eight days, and the Paynes and their co-litigants lost. Six days later, run down, worn out, ravaged by dietary and drinking excesses, the aftermath of the yaws he had contracted in the Solomon Islands and the arsenical drugs he took to cure them, Jack London died. He had taken a heavy, if not lethal, dose of morphine, became comatose, and never wakened. Whether he was a suicide or had only sought relief from the agony of his renal colic is not known, but the most convincing argument is that he did not premeditate his death.[9]

Andrew Sinclair's judgment is probably as close to the truth as is possible at this distance: "Jack's self-destruction did not take place that night. He had been slowly destroying himself for a decade. . ."[10]

Edward Biron Payne died in 1923, at the age of 75, soon after the disastrous Berkeley fire which destroyed hundreds of homes, including his and Ninetta's. Two book manuscripts were consumed in the fire at the Payne home, one of them titled *The Soul of Jack London,* but a carbon copy of this work was later found, and in 1926 it was published in England.

The Soul of Jack London, a remarkable piece of curiosa, is a grandiloquent concoction of biography, philosophy, and metaphysics which has, as its most important and only really interesting feature, a long account of a psychic's "contact" with Jack London in 1921 and London's "communications" from Beyond with the world and with his friends left behind. Chief among those "friends," as might be predicted, were Ninetta and Edward Payne.

---

[9] Russ Kingman, *A Pictorial Life of Jack London,* pp. 272–74.

[10] Sinclair, p. 242.

"Mother Mine" — Ninetta Eames Payne.

The book relates that the Paynes wrote a letter to London in March 1921, which was relayed to the deceased author by the psychic. In their letter, Ninetta and her husband faulted Jack for succumbing to the alcoholic grip of John Barleycorn but wished him well in his struggle to purge himself of his sins and his search "to merit the eternal gifts and endowments."[11] London's "answer," relayed through the medium, contained the words "I wronged you — I wronged others. The list is long."[12] And in another communication, asked if he had a message for the Paynes, London is supposed to have responded, "I who have come send this word. Love of my soul to their souls in endless communion."[13]

Jack London, who was not above writing lines of soporific melodrama on occasion, would have cringed to have had such utterances ascribed to him in life, and it is virtually impossible to avoid the conclusion reached by his biographer Richard O'Connor:

Jack had always dealt harshly with Payne's views. . . . In *The Soul of Jack London,* published in London ten years after his death, Payne and Aunt Netta obtained their posthumous revenge. . . . Even in the great beyond, the way the Paynes told it, Jack was not spared the treacly reproaches of "Mother Mine."[14]

With this background, we now examine Conan Doyle's involvement with Payne's book and its curious revelations.

In the post-World War I era, Sir Arthur had become passionately devoted to psychic phenomena — spiritualism, ghosts, fairies, telepathy, clairvoyance, and all the substrata of the paranormal — so much so, it has been said, that he sacrificed a

---

[11] Payne, pp. 104–9.

[12] *Ibid.,* p. 111.

[13] *Ibid.,* p. 95.

[14] Richard O'Connor, *Jack London: A Biography,* p. 399.

Edward Biron Payne.

peerage for his sometimes embarrassing public pronouncements on the subject.[15]

In *The Edge of the Unknown,* Doyle wrote, just a few months before his own death:

We who believe in the psychic revelation, and who appreciate that a perception of these things is of the utmost importance, certainly have hurled ourselves against the obstinacy of our time. Possibly we have allowed some of our lives to be gnawed away in what, for the moment, seemed a vain and thankless quest. Only the future can show whether the sacrifice was worth it. Personally I think it was.[16]

Sir Arthur read *The Soul of Jack London* in manuscript, and on July 1, 1925, from his "Windlesham" home in Crowborough, Sussex, wrote a moving letter which served as a preface when the book was published the following year. He believed that the book contained "an extraordinarily lucid analysis of the man and his work" and predicted that it would "hold a place of its own—a decisive place" in future discussions of London's work and character. He expressed a natural and special interest in the psychic portions of the manuscript and said that the best evidence of the authenticity of the "contact" made with London was "the style of those extracts which are quoted." He expressed no surprise over Jack London's "reappearance" and said, "I was aware that a strong soul dying prematurely with many earth interests in its thoughts, would be very likely to come back." Sir Arthur said he was so convinced that a man "of great resolution and dynamic force" such as London *would* reappear that he wrote to London's widow, shortly after her husband's death, of "the overwhelming evidence of such possibility, and the fact that of all men her husband was the most likely to take advantage of it if the right conditions were afforded." Finally, Doyle wrote of his hope that the book would be published, serving as "one more brick in the huge monument of proof which is now growing so

---

[15] Michael and Mollie Hardwick, *The Man Who Was Sherlock Holmes,* p. 86. The authors also credit Sir Arthur's plea for clemency in the case of Roger Casement (hanged for high treason on August 3, 1916) as a factor in the loss of the baronetcy.

[16] Arthur Conan Doyle, *The Edge of the Unknown,* p. (7).

large, that even the blindest of mankind can hardly make a pretense of not recognizing it."[17]

In *The Edge of the Unknown,* Sir Arthur traced his acquaintanceship with the Payne-London revelations, quoted from *The Soul of Jack London,* and concluded:

Alas, Jack, the world is too busy with its games and its pleasures, too immersed in its wooden creeds and its petrified religions, to give ear to what you have learned. They, like you, will only realize when it is too late. . . . I accept Jack London's return as being a genuine one. I can see no other possible conclusion.[18]

---

[17] Payne, Appendix, pp. 133–36. Sir Arthur's Preface in the first, British, edition became the Appendix in the second, American, edition.

[18] Doyle, p. 103.

"From the color in her cheeks, Grief concluded that she had not been long in the tropics." A bit of deduction from "A Little Account with Swithin Hall" (A SON OF THE SUN, 1912), illustrated by Anton Otto Fischer, whose work London called "the best drawings for my stories I have ever seen."

4 Salutes to Sherlock

JACK LONDON, for all the fecundity of ideas in his fiction and the sheer bulk of it, wrote no detective stories in the common sense, though he came close on occasion, such as in his "The Master of Mystery" (1902).[1]

This amusing tale concerns an Alaskan Thlinket Indian's missing blankets and the efforts of two tribal medicine men to locate them. One shaman, Klok-No-Ton, imported from a neighboring village, is a fearsome creature whose methods of flushing out a thief consist of torture, curses, and exorcism. The Thlinket's own shaman, Scundoo, temporarily in disrepute for inaccurately predicting a south wind that would help the tribal journey to a nearby *potlatch* (a ceremonial occasion in which gifts are bestowed from tribe to tribe), is cleverer — something of a detective and a student of human nature. He has a suspect in mind, one Sime, who Scundoo knows will be unmoved by Klok-No-Ton's scare tactics. Scundoo prepares a trap. He takes a soot-blackened pot in the house of Hooniah, whose blankets have been stolen, and places under the overturned vessel a raven — "diviner of mystery and seer of things." That night, each of the Thlinket tribesmen files past the pot and lays a hand upon it. Scundoo warns that the raven will make an outcry "when the hand of the evil-doer is nigh him." After all have emerged from Hooniah's house, a fire is lighted and Scundoo announces, "Let every man, woman, and child, now and at once, hold their hands well up above their heads!" This is done, and soon all eyes come to rest upon Sime. Every hand but his is black with soot, "and he was guiltless of the smirch of Hooniah's pot."

---

[1] *Out West* magazine, September 1902, included in *Children of the Frost*. The story was reprinted in *Ellery Queen's Mystery Magazine,* June 1954.

Even considering this primitive, if delightful, piece of sleuth-
ing, London wrote no formal detective stories. As we shall see,
he once gave some momentary thought to writing a series of
police tales containing a continuing character inspired by the
great Baker Street personage, but, unfortunately for future
generations, and for Sinclair Lewis, this series never materialized.
Still, a good many of London's stories contain mysteries, and
the few passages of detection he did incorporate into his work
are purely Sherlockian in character. As with Peter Gee's monologue in "A Goboto Night," they are, in a word, *touches* of
Holmes.

In yet another of the David Grief adventures, contained in the
1912 collection *A Son of the Sun,* Grief uses his own deductive
powers to foil an imposter.

The story is "A Little Account with Swithin Hall,"[2] in which
Grief's schooner *Uncle Toby* is caught in hurricane weather in
the Leu-Leu atolls. Land is sighted and turns out to be the
mysterious island belonging to Swithin Hall, a dot of land in a
maze of atolls inhabited by a man who some years before had
swindled and financially ruined a member of Grief's crew.
Swithin Hall's bungalow on the island contains lavish furnish-
ings—a living room covered with fine Samoan mats, couches, a
billiard table, sewing materials, and French embroidery. The
library is filled with the works of Tolstoy, Turgenieff, Gorky,
Cooper, Twain, Hugo, Zola, Sue, Flaubert, Schopenhauer,
Krafft-Ebbing, and other classics.

From their first encounter, Grief is suspicious of the man who
introduces himself as Swithin Hall, a large, heavily-built, round-
faced man carrying a long-barreled Colt revolver. Back on the
Uncle Toby, Grief tells his mate: "That man ashore there never
bought the books on the shelves. . . . He's got a surface flow of
suavity, but he's rough as a hoe-rasp underneath." Grief is also
dubious of "Hall's" crew on the island (one of whom is named
"Watson")—"real sea-dogs, middle-aged, marred and battered,
tough as rusty wrought-iron nails and twice as dangerous; real
ugly customers, with guns in the belts." But the clincher for

---

[2] *Saturday Evening Post,* September 2, 1911; collected in *A Son of the
Sun.*

Grief is "Hall's" indifferent play at the billiards table. The real Swithin Hall is a master of the game and a legend in the islands.

The story, a neat tale of the stinging of a con-man, ends with Grief escorting the fake Swithin Hall from the island along with enough pearls from Hall's private lagoon to repay the $60,000 swindled from Grief's shipmate.

An even more telling touch of Sherlock, *à la* "A Scandal in Bohemia," is to be found in London's "The Mistake of Creation,"[3] one of the 1912 series of Yukon stories involving the characters Smoke Bellew and his sidekick Shorty. Smoke and Shorty are in the Nordbeska River country when they find a number of human corpses along the trail. Smoke deduces that they have committed suicide: "They're fat," he tells Shorty—a sort of back-country Watson. "That means no famine. They've not struck it rich, else they wouldn't have committed suicide. . . . There are no tracks besides their own, and each is powder-burned."

Further along the trail, they find a large encampment of over twenty cabins, "the Laura Sibley outfit" from Los Angeles. (London seems to have taken delight in making the weakling head of the expedition, Laura Sibley, a clairvoyant, vegetarian, sect-leader.) In every cabin they visit, Smoke and Shorty find groaning, desperately ill men and women, so lethargic they cannot move from their bunks, much less help one another. All have been stricken with scurvy, and Smoke says it is raw potatoes, the best anti-scorbutic of them all, that is missing from their diet. The evaporated, dry potatoes in the Sibley expedition stores do not work in warding off the disease.

One man and one alone of the Sibley outfit seems free of the sickness. He is Amos Wentworth, a man hated by the entire camp and, soon after meeting him, by both Smoke and Shorty. Wentworth keeps to his cabin, and Smoke suspects he is protecting a cache of potatoes there. This is confirmed when Smoke is able to buy a single potato from Wentworth for $1,000 in gold dust. But appealing to Wentworth's humanity has no effect, nor does breaking into his cabin and tearing it apart searching for

---

[3] *Cosmopolitan,* February 1912; collected in *Smoke Bellew.*

the potato cache, nor Shorty's administration of a brutal beating to the man he labels "that mistake of creation."

The two decide to burn Wentworth's cabin and watch the result. Says Smoke:

"I always told you, Shorty, that a deficient acquaintance with literature was a handicap, even in the Klondike. Now what we're going to do came out of a book. I read it when I was a kid, and it will work."

What book? A collection of Poe's tales containing "The Purloined Letter"? But Dupin was lucky in that one: a gunshot enabled him to switch a clever forgery for the letter he sought. No, the book Smoke Bellew read "when he was a kid" had appeared only five years before he made use of it. It was *The Adventures of Sherlock Holmes* (1892), and the story was "A Scandal in Bohemia," wherein Holmes is engaged by the King of Bohemia to obtain a certain indiscreet photograph from Irene Adler. Holmes employs a disguise as a clergyman, a little fake blood, Watson, and a smoke rocket. As he tells Watson later:

"When a woman thinks that her house is on fire, her instinct is at once to rush to the thing which she values most. It is a perfectly overpowering impulse, and I have more than once taken advantage of it."

Smoke and Shorty set fire to Amos Wentworth's cabin, and the infamous potato-miser rushes out of his room, then back in, emerging with his treasure, a heavy sack of potatoes. The two men pounce on Wentworth, beat him severely, and commandeer the life-saving vegetables. The Sibley camp is saved, Wentworth is an outcast, begging to accompany Smoke and Shorty to Dawson, as he does not know the ways of travel in the Klondike. Says Shorty:

"I'm a worm, a maggot, a brother to the pollywog an' child of the blow-fly. I ain't afraid or ashamed of nothin' that creeps or crawls or stinks. But travel with that mistake of creation! Go 'way, man. I ain't proud, but you turn my stomach. . . . I hope a skunk bites you an' you get howlin' hydrophoby."

Smoke Bellew and his sidekick Shorty confront Amos Went-worth after Smoke has used the fire ploy from "A Scandal in Bohemia" to trick Wentworth into revealing his cache of potatoes. Illustration by Anton Otto Fischer from COSMOPOLITAN, *February 1912. Reproduced by permission.*

In the 1892 Sherlock Holmes story "Silver Blaze," in which England's most famous racehorse has been kidnapped and his trainer murdered, occurs the best example of what Father Ronald Knox called the *Sherlockismus* — the theatrical, paradoxical epigram. The speakers are, in turn, Inspector Gregory and Holmes:

> "Is there any other point to which you would draw my attention?"
> "To the curious incident of the dog in the night-time."
> "The dog did nothing in the night-time."
> "That was the curious incident," remarked Sherlock Holmes.

In one of his posthumously-published books, *Jerry of the Islands,*[4] there is a brief incident, dealing with the island dog Jerry, that is plainly-labeled Holmes and reminiscent of the "Silver Blaze" *Sherlockismus.*

In Chapter 20 of the novel, Jerry is rescued after a hair-raising series of adventures by the American couple Villa and Harley Kennan, who are on a world cruise in their schooner *Ariel.* Both the Kennans recognize Jerry as "a white man's dog," and not a native islander, but Villa maintains she has the crowning proof of it.

> "The dog carries the evidence around with him."
> Harley looked Jerry over carefully.
> "Indisputable evidence," she insisted.
> After another prolonged scrutiny, Kennan shook his head. "Blamed if I can see anything so indisputable as to leave conjecture out."
> "The tail," his wife gurgled. "Surely the natives do not bob the tails of their dogs."

Then, addressing the native boy Johnny in the "beche-de-mer" pidgin English employed to communicate with the islanders, Villa continues:

> "Do they, Johnny? Do black man stop along Malaita chop'm off tail belong dog?"
> "No chop'm off," Johnny agreed. "Mister Haggin alone Meringe he chop'm off. My word, he chop'm off that fella tail, you bet."

---

[4] Published serially in *Cosmopolitan,* January–April 1917.

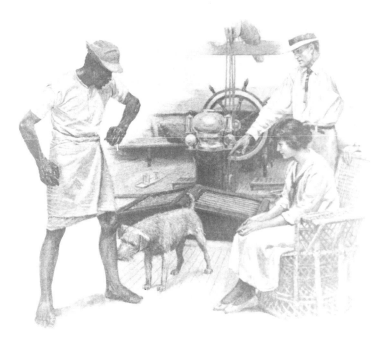

Villa and Harley Kennan take note of the evidence that Jerry is a "white man's dog." Illustration by Anton Otto Fischer from COSMOPOLITAN, *April 1917. Reproduced by permission.*

"Then he's the sole survivor of the *Arangi,*" Villa Kennan concluded. "Don't you agree, Mr. Sherlock Holmes Kennan?"

"I salute you, Mrs. S. Holmes," her husband acknowledged gallantly.

There is another example of plainly-labeled Holmes in London's 1914 novel *The Mutiny of the Elsinore.*[5] In Chapter 32 occurs a minor cabin mystery in which the contents of a gallon can of wood alcohol gradually disappears. The episode contains the explicit debt to Holmes and Watson but would have been unmistakable in any event. London writes that the steward and his partner in detection "compared notes and then made of themselves a Sherlock Holmes and Dr. Watson."

First they gauged the daily diminution of alcohol. Next they gauged it several times daily, and learned that the diminution, when it occurred, was first apparent immediately after meal-time. This focused their attention on two suspects — the second mate and the carpenter, who alone ate in the after-room. The rest was easy. Whenever Mr. Mellaire arrived ahead of the carpenter, the more alcohol was missing. When they arrived together, the alcohol was undisturbed. The carpenter was never alone in the room. The syllogism was complete.

The methodology, it must be admitted, is perhaps more reminiscent of Captain Queeg than of Sherlock Holmes!

As explicitly labeled as is the foregoing is the dialogue which takes place in Chapter 35 of London's *The Sea Wolf* (1904)[6] between Humphrey Van Weyden and Maud Brewster, castaways on Endeavor Island. Says the prim Humphrey to the prim Maud:

"Look at those three-cornered tears. And such a waist! It would not require a Sherlock Holmes to deduce that you have been cooking over a camp-fire, to say nothing of trying out seal-blubber."

---

[5] Published serially in *Hearst's* magazine, November 1913–August 1914.

[6] Published serially in the *Century* magazine, January–November 1904.

Humphrey Van Weyden and Maud Brewster on Endeavor Island, where he remarks on her "draggled skirts" and deduces she has been cooking over a camp-fire. Illustration by W. J. Aylward for THE SEA WOLF *(1904).*

Sinclair Lewis and his Carmel colony friends in January 1909. Standing: Lewis, Alice MacGowan, and William Rose Benét. Seated: Grace MacGowan Cook and Miss Scannel, the "spectacularly incompetent" secretary whom Lewis was hired to replace.

5 The Singular Adventure of
Hal Lewis's Plots

In examining Jack London's indebtedness to Conan Doyle, and in particular to Doyle's Sherlock Holmes, the most tantalizing aspect of the story is the curious role played in it by Sinclair Lewis.

In the spring of 1910, "Hal" Lewis was preparing to leave Carmel-by-the-Sea, the little Bohemia-like settlement south of Monterey Bay. Here he shared a small cottage with poet William Rose Benét while working as part-time secretary to the well-known writers of the day, Alice MacGowan and Grace MacGowan Cooke. Lewis, as prolific a writer as London, was at the beginning of his auspicious career and, since earning his A.B. degree at Yale in 1907, had continually published, earning small sums for sales to *Youth's Companion, Woman's Home Companion, Smart Set, Century,* and many other periodicals, as well as for newspaper work on the San Francisco *Bulletin* and the Waterloo (Iowa) *Daily Courier.*

As a plot deviser, Lewis's invention was astonishing. He had brought with him to Carmel a trunk packed with notes and newspaper clippings together with an enormous plot file. His friend Benét remembered Lewis's ability to reel off impromptu stories as the two of them tramped the California coast.[1]

His biographer Mark Schorer has said that Lewis's problem was "a lack of imaginative focus and an inability to develop fictional situations either fully or dramatically."[2]

Jack London had precisely the opposite problem. Writing furiously to maintain his astronomical income, he admitted his

---

[1] Mark Schorer, *Sinclair Lewis,* pp. 164–65.

[2] *Ibid.,* p. 164.

aridity of *ideas* for new stories. Once he had the plot, execution posed no hindrance. He wrote his daily "stint" of 1,000 words as regularly as clockwork, but the system required constant fueling with *ideas*.

It was fateful that Lewis and London would meet at this time. Lewis had been in the audience at Yale in 1906, when London lectured the students there on the Socialist revolution in America, and was among those outraged at the conduct of his fellow students — the booing, feet-stamping and laughing. Lewis may have been among those present afterward when London answered questions for two hours in a dormitory filled with generally hostile interrogators. Now, four years later, Lewis still had a sense of awe about Jack London and referred to him on occasion as "Master."[3]

London came to Carmel in March 1910 to visit his poet-friend George Sterling, and, in the close-knit group that formed the early-day Carmel "colony," he came into close contact with Lewis. The two apparently hit it off and spent one entire night in Sterling's cottage going through Lewis's plot file. The result was the sale to London of fourteen short-story plots for $70 cash. Lewis used the money to buy a ticket to Washington, D.C., where he went to work on the *Volta Review,* a journal devoted to teaching the deaf to speak.[4]

Six months later, London wrote Lewis and asked for more. Lewis responded by sending twenty-three story ideas, of which London selected nine and sent a check for $52.50, returning the balance of them, including one ambitious idea for a series of stories to be called collectively *The World Police.*

Without exception, the stories Jack London wrote from the Lewis plots were painfully inferior. The only complete book, a novelette, derived from this arrangement was *The Abysmal Brute* (1913), and, although London professed pride in this thin

---

[3] *Ibid.,* p. 104.

[4] Franklin Walker, *The Seacoast of Bohemia,* pp. 86–89. Other sources for the singular episode of the Lewis plots include: Franklin Walker, "Jack London's Use of Sinclair Lewis Plots," *Huntington Library Quarterly,* November 1953, pp. 59–74; Hendricks and Shepard, pp. 483–89; and Schorer, pp. 166–67.

prize-fight tale, as he did of virtually all his worst work, it is exceedingly contrived and melodramatic. Of the three published short stories based on Lewis plots—"The Prodigal Father," "Winged Blackmail," and "When the World Was Young"[5]—none is worthy of Jack London's by-line, nor that of Sinclair Lewis, for that matter.

In his dealings with Lewis, there were two instances, one a plot purchased, the other a plot rejected, of special interest in this study of the London-Conan Doyle literary kinship.

Among the fourteen story outlines London purchased from Lewis on March 11, 1910, was the synopsis for a work to be called *The Assassination Bureau, Ltd.* The outline concerned a sort of international Murder, Inc., operated by a high-minded intellectual who ordered murders carried out only if it could be proven to his satisfaction that the proposed victim deserved to die. London worked up 20,000 words of this, then threw up his hands in despair. He could think of no satisfactory ending for it, and, although Lewis himself drew up an elaborate summary for concluding the story, London apparently rejected the idea.[6] London's wife Charmian, something of a writer herself, also devised an ending, as, eventually, did Jack himself, but neither was used.

The Assassination Bureau, Ltd. was completed by Robert L. Fish and published in 1963. The McGraw-Hill book contained details of both Jack's and Charmian's proposed endings for the story, but neither was employed by Fish. Perhaps no writer could have completed the book more satisfactorily nor imitated London's style more expertly. In addition to being a winner of the Edgar Allan Poe Award from the Mystery Writers of America for his novels, he is known to all students of the Baker Street saga for his delightful burlesques featuring Schlock Homes and Dr. Watney.

The London-Fish novel was the basis for the 1969 film *The Assassination Bureau,* directed by Basil Dearden and starring Diana Rigg, Oliver Reed, Telly Savalas, and Curt Jurgens. It

---

[5] The first may be found in the collection *The Turtles of Tasman,* the other two in *The Night Born.*

[6] O'Connor, p. 302.

was, Fish wrote, "a lovely little spoof which had as much to do with the book as it did with Anne of Green Gables."[7]

We are concerned here, however, with the first two-thirds of the book, the portion written by Jack London himself. It contains a number of elements springing unquestionably from London's admiration of Sherlock Holmes and his methods, as well as for Holmes's most famous nemesis, Professor Moriarty, and *his* methods. In *The Assassination Bureau, Ltd.,* the pursuit of Ivan Dragomiloff, founder of the Bureau, by his own agents — a cleverly calculated, anticipating-his-next-move chase — clearly recalls Conan Doyle's breathtaking scenes in which Holmes and Moriarty were on one another's heels *en route* to the fatal encounter at Reichenbach Falls. Moreover, the drawing-room conversations between Dragomiloff and Winter Hall, the hero of the story, are reminiscent of those treasured, quiet times in their Baker Street lodgings, when Holmes would curl up in his chair, wreathed in the vapors of his pipe, place his fingertips together, and say something profound to the phlegmatic Watson, the doctor looking up from reading one of Clark Russell's fine sea stories.

An example is this exchange between Dragomiloff and Hall:

Dragomiloff laced and interlaced his strong, lean fingers and meditated for further answer. "I might explain that we conduct our trade with a greater measure of ethics than our clients bring to us."

"Ethics!" Hall burst into laughter.

"Yes, precisely; and I'll admit it sounds funny in connection with an Assassination Bureau."

"Is that what you call it?"

"One name is as good as another," the head of the Bureau went on imperturbably. "But you will find, in patronizing us, a keener, a more rigid standard of right-dealing than in the business world. I saw the need of that at the start. It was imperative."[8]

Dragomiloff, while more a brother of Moriarty than of Holmes, possesses characteristics of each, while Hall is merely a fop. Both, however, are intellectuals, and their conversational

---

[7] Letter to D.L.W., June 27, 1974.

[8] Jack London and Robert L. Fish, *The Assassination Bureau, Ltd.,* pp. 30–31.

The jacket for the 1963 McGraw-Hill printing of London's unfinished THE ASSASSINATION BUREAU, LTD., *"completed by Robert L. Fish from notes by Jack London." Jacket design by Willi Baum.*

fencing makes a more accurate contrast if one imagines Moriarty opposite Holmes in the Baker Street sitting-room.

Six months after *The Assassination Bureau, Ltd.* plot was purchased, Lewis sent another batch of story ideas at London's request. Concerning us here is one of those which London rejected. Had he pursued it, especially in the manner prescribed by Lewis, studies of London as a writer of detective fiction would long ago have been undertaken.

The plot London returned had to do with a series of stories under the collective title *The World Police*. Lewis rarely asked for more than $15 per plot, most often $5, but had a $40 price tag on the *World Police* idea. In his explanatory letter accompanying the outline, Lewis wrote:

I've been for years watching out for a series. That's where Conan Doyle made his stake—starting the Sherlock Holmes series; a bunch of stories which, each singly, would be lost; but which, unified by the central figure of Sherlock Holmes, made Conan Doyle all he is today. So in a lesser degree with Barr's Lord Stanleigh stories; Hornung's Raffles series; Leblanc's Arsene Lupin tales, and a hundred other instances. . . . The series would not be touched till you really feel acquainted with the big central figure, the man who is the series; everything about him from his ideas on matrimony up to his brand of tobacco. He need not—should not, and, with you writing, would not—be in the least like Sherlock Holmes but Holmes offers suggestions nevertheless.

And, in a partly-prophetic last paragraph of his letter—this was, remember, October 1910—Lewis wrote:

This series is supposed to take place after the great world war of Germany and Japan vs. U.S. and England has ended in a world peace. It might be dated after the coming of Socialism, but I doubt it, because that regime would probably result in the formation of a world nation, and it's better for the series to have seperate nations with which the world police toy.

London's reply to this idea was negatively succinct:

I didn't care to tackle the World Police (which is a splendid series) because I am long on splendid novel-motifs of my own, which require only time and relaxed financial pressure for me to put through.[9]

---

[9] Harry E. Maule and Melville Caine (eds.), *The Man from Main Street,* pp. 123–25.

The London-Lewis "collaboration," a bizarre footnote in American literary history, was thus short-lived and essentially non-productive. But in two remarkable instances within that collaboration, one unfinished but attempted, the other "a splendid series" he declined to tackle, London's debt to Conan Doyle was reaffirmed.

To close this extraordinary episode, it is worthwhile to note that Sinclair Lewis, in a letter to Harvey Taylor, literary executor of the Jack London estate in the early 1930s, wrote of his association with London this way: "It was to me a very exciting and helpful thing to be permitted to suggest fresh slants on his own wisdom."[10]

And looking at the association more than two decades later, Mary Austin (the author of *The Land of Little Rain, Isidro, Lands of the Sun* and many other books), who had been instrumental in the founding of the Carmel colony and who knew both London and Lewis, wrote in her autobiography:

I have always suspected that Jack's buying of plots for short stories from any writer with more plots than places to bestow them was chiefly a generous camouflage for help that could not be asked or given otherwise."[11]

---

[10] Kingman, p. 160.

[11] Mary Austin, *Earth Horizon,* p. 304.

Sir Arthur and Lady Doyle, left, visiting with Mary Pickford and Douglas Fairbanks on the set of ROSITA.

6 The Kinship

CONAN DOYLE was sixty-three when, in the spring of 1923, he made his final trip to America, accompanied by Lady Doyle and their three children. He lectured at Carnegie Hall on April 16 and then traveled westward to Denver—where he saw his (and Jack London's) friend Harry Houdini perform at the Orpheum Theatre—thence to San Diego and Los Angeles, speaking on the single topic important to him in his late life: spiritualism. The Doyles had a grand time in southern California, watching the filming of the Mary Pickford movie *Rosita,* Sir Arthur bouncing little Jackie Coogan on his knee, attending séances, and bantering with reporters who trailed him doggedly. [1]

The entourage traveled on to San Francisco from Hollywood. Jack London had died six and a half years earlier, his ashes reposing under a huge, reddish, granite boulder on his ranch in the Valley of the Moon, to the north of the city of his birth.

"I have considered Jack London my greatest American contemporary in the world of letters," Doyle said in an interview in the San Francisco *Chronicle* published on May 31, 1923. "He got to the root of things, and he expressed himself wonderfully."

What a pity the two never met! They might have, as early as 1902, when London was in London, living amongst the people of the East End abyss while Conan Doyle was becoming Sir Arthur. Better yet, they might have met in 1910, if Doyle had accepted Tex Rickard's invitation to come to Reno, Nevada and serve as referee in the heavyweight championship fight between Jack Johnson and the "Great White Hope," Jim Jeffries. Sir Arthur was excited over the prospect at first, but cooler reason

---

[1] Charles Higham, *The Adventures of Conan Doyle,* pp. 296-99; Howard Lachtman, "When Conan Doyle Came to California," *Pacific Historian,* Spring 1978, pp. 28-37.

prevailed: He had no business getting involved in the heated racial issue that clouded the fight, and he declined the offer.[2]

Jack London was there, covering the fight for the New York *Herald*.

Prize-fighting! If Jack London had been alive in 1923, he and Doyle would have tramped the Beauty Ranch and enjoyed many an hour of talk about this subject they loved. It would have been an amusing Mutt-and-Jeff scene: Sir Arthur stood six-foot-four and 230 or so pounds, Jack about five-seven and thick around the middle. But both had been amateur boxers. Doyle had taken his old, worn boxing gloves in his kit when he sailed on the *Hope* back in '80 and for years had a sparring partner come twice a week to Windlesham to work out with him. London loved to put on the gloves and spar with all comers—even his athletic wife, Charmian.

Both had written of the prize ring, too. Doyle's *Rodney Stone* (1896) was a Regency-era prize-fight story with a Beau Brummel-type dandy hero who becomes a "man" at the end. He had even written a dramatization of *Rodney Stone,* titled *The House of Temperley* (1910), which had a great prize-fight scene he demanded be done authentically and realistically. The play had closed early, opening, as it unfortunately did, on the eve of King Edward VII's death.[3] And there were such fine Doyle boxing stories as "The Croxley Master" (1899), and of course such episodes as Holmes, an accomplished pugilist, knocking out the villainous Jack Woodley with a hard left in the adventure of "The Solitary Cyclist" (1904):

"He had a fine flow of language, and his adjectives were very vigorous. He ended a string of abuse by a vicious back-hander, which I failed to entirely avoid. The next few minutes were delicious. It was a straight left against a slogging ruffian. I emerged as you see me. Mr. Woodley went home in a cart."

London's prize-fight works were no less impressive; indeed, in two instances at least, were more impressive. His "A Piece of Steak" (1909) and "The Mexican" (1911) are superb tales of the

---

[2] Carr, p. 298.   [3] *Ibid.,* pp. 300–3.

Jack and Charmian often put the gloves on for a backyard sparring session at their home in Glen Ellen, California.

prize ring, frequently anthologized to this day. He also wrote two short boxing novels, *The Game* (1905) and the one based on a Sinclair Lewis plot, *The Abysmal Brute* (1913).

Doyle, no doubt, would have steered the conversation with London as often as possible to the subject of spiritualism. London professed utter disbelief and disgust with all of it. He had been weaned on spiritualism and had rejected it in boyhood. Yet, throughout his writing career, like Conan Doyle, Jack London was drawn again and again to fantasy, stories of strange and unearthly events, the unexplainable, and the unknowable.

Conan Doyle, toward the end of his life, converted his Professor George Edward Challenger to spiritualism in *The Land of Mist* (1926) and wrote of the rediscovery of Atlantis in *The Maracot Deep* (1929). These were but extensions of the kind of scientific romance he had written as early as 1892, in *The Doings of Raffles Haw,* wherein a gold-maker is disenchanted with philanthropy and destroys his machine and himself in the process, and which he carried to the heights in the Challenger novels *The Lost World* (1912) and *The Poison Belt* (1913) and in that remarkably prescient story, "Danger!" written on the eve of World War I, in which Doyle warned of submarine attacks on merchant shipping.

Jack London, toward the end of his life, returned to the fantasy "motif" (one of his favorite words) in "The Red One," a story he completed in Hawaii in May 1916 but which was posthumously published (1918). In this haunting tale, London struck a note of cosmic mystery that must have appealed greatly to Conan Doyle. It is the story of a scientist who is taken prisoner by head-hunting natives on Guadalcanal. In captivity he continues to seek the source of the resonant bell-sound he hears periodically and which he likens to "the mighty cry of some Titan of the Elder World vexed with misery or wrath." He sacrifices his life to see the Red One — an enormous reddish-colored sphere, an interstellar visitor landed on the island ages past, deified by the natives, who have carpeted the jungle clearing upon which it rests with the bones of human sacrifices. The eerie sound emanating from it is produced through the agency of a giant tree-trunk, a kingpost carved with dynasties of gods, suspended on ropes and driven against the sphere's strangely coruscating surface.

In 1899, London wrote "A Thousand Deaths," in which a young man is revived from drowning and held captive on a madman's yacht, where he becomes a guinea pig in a series of grotesque revivification experiments. To escape, the prisoner sets up a powerful electrical field and disintegrates his captors. In 1892, Doyle had written a story titled "The Los Amigos Fiasco," in which an experimental electric chair supercharges a criminal instead of executing him.

Doyle had his dinosaurs on the South American plateau of *The Lost World,* London his mastodon in "A Relic of the Pliocene" (1901) and his prehistoric world of "The Strength of the Strong" (1911) and his atavistic dream novel *Before Adam* (1907). Doyle wrote in *The Poison Belt* of the earth entering a poisonous stream high in the ether which spells the doom of mankind; London's *The Scarlet Plague* (1915) tells of the mysterious pandemic plague of 2013 devastating earth and how, sixty years later, survivors and their progeny are beginning to crawl back from savagery. Doyle's "Danger!" foretold of submarine warfare, London's "The Unparalleled Invasion" (1910) foretold of bacteriological warfare.

Both were sailors, boxers, and, in their separate manners, mystics.

But of all the trace elements of Conan Doyle in Jack London's work and vice-versa, of the occasional similarities in their vastly different characters, life-styles, and careers, the unifying element of their kinship is Sherlock Holmes. There can be little question that London was attracted to Holmes, not only because of the infectious charm and popularity of the stories, but because he admired the incisively analytical and determinedly rationalistic mind of Holmes. It was the kind of mind Jack London admired but did not always have.

There is a final paradox in this, the most important element of the London-Doyle kinship, suggested by Dr. Howard Lachtman,[4] the distinguished London scholar. Sherlock Holmes, a fictitious character who has come to life in the minds of generations of readers, stands in contrast to Jack London, a man who has taken on the qualities of a fictional creation—perhaps one of his

---

[4] Letter to D.L.W., April 20, 1980.

Jack London in 1914.

own fabrication; a man about whom it is said: "His own life story, his consciously created legend, was an even greater artistic work than any he committed to paper."[5] Or, as Andrew Sinclair put it: "Jack London lived nine lives and wrote more than fifty books and founded a ranch and died at forty. A man like that is worth his own myths."[6] Or, in the words of London scholar Earle Labor:

A literary idol who became a national legend before he reached the age of thirty. . . . If in the final analysis, Jack London still eludes us, perhaps it is only fitting and proper. After all, he is one of our great folk heroes, and our avatars are traditionally invested with certain mysteries."[7]

The last sentence is also an eloquent description of Sherlock Holmes.

The man whose work London so admired and which so inspired him should have the final word. Conan Doyle, in a letter written on July 1, 1925 from Crowborough to the London spiritualist Miss F. R. Scatcherd, said:

Jack London was ranked by many critics during his lifetime as a mere writer of sensations, but I was always of the opinion that he really had such an equipment of mind, energy and actual experience as few authors have had the good fortune to possess. I discerned also that in his deep and complex nature, which different forces were fighting to control, there was a purely mental one which led him to the darkness of materialism, and an idealistic one which urged him to the heights. I am sure that even now his work has not received its full recognition and that anything concerning him will be of great interest in days to come.[8]

[5] O'Connor, p. 401.

[6] Sinclair, p. 252.

[7] Earle Labor, *Jack London,* p. 150.

[8] Payne, p. 133.

Bibliography

Austin, Mary. *Earth Horizon.* New York: Houghton Mifflin, 1932.

Barltrop, Robert. *Jack London: The Man, the Writer, the Rebel.* London: Pluto Press, 1976.

Carr, John Dickson. *The Life of Sir Arthur Conan Doyle.* New York: Vintage Books, 1975. (Originally published by Harper & Row, 1949.)

Doyle, Arthur Conan. *The Edge of the Unknown.* New York: G. P. Putnam's Sons, 1930.

Foner, Philip, ed. *Jack London: American Rebel.* New York: The Citadel Press, 1947.

Hardwick, Michael and Mollie. *The Man Who Was Sherlock Holmes.* Garden City: Doubleday & Co., 1964.

Hendricks, King and Irving Shepard, eds. *Letters from Jack London.* New York: Odyssey Press, 1965.

Higham, Charles. *The Adventures of Conan Doyle.* New York: Norton, 1976.

Kingman, Russ. *A Pictorial Life of Jack London.* New York: Crown, 1980.

Labor, Earle. *Jack London.* New York: Twayne Publishers, 1974.

London, Charmian K. *The Book of Jack London.* Two volumes. New York: The Century Co., 1920.

London, Joan. *Jack London and His Times.* New York: Doubleday, 1939.

Maule, Harry E. and Melville Caine, eds. *The Man from Main Street.* New York: Random House, 1953.

Nordon, Pierre. *Conan Doyle*. New York: Holt, Rinehart & Winston, 1967.

O'Connor, Richard. *Jack London: A Biography*. Boston: Little, Brown, 1964.

Payne, Edward B. *The Soul of Jack London*. Kingsport, Tenn.: Southern Publishers, 1933.

Schorer, Mark. *Sinclair Lewis: An American Life*. New York: McGraw-Hill, 1961.

Shepard, Irving, ed. *Jack London's Tales of Adventure*. Garden City: Doubleday, 1956.

Sinclair, Andrew. *Jack*. New York: Harper & Row, 1977.

Stone, Irving. *Sailor on Horseback*. Cambridge, Mass.: Houghton Mifflin, 1936.

Tracy, Jack. *Conan Doyle and the Latter-Day Saints*. Bloomington, Ind.: Gaslight Publications, 1979.

Walker, Dale L. *The Alien Worlds of Jack London*. Grand Rapids, Mich.: Wolf House Books, 1973.

Walker, Dale L. *Curious Fragments: Jack London's Tales of Fantasy Fiction*. Port Washington, N.Y.: Kennikat Press, 1975.

Walker, Franklin. *Jack London and the Klondike*. San Marino, Calif.: Huntington Library, 1966.

Walker, Franklin. *The Seacoast of Bohemia*. Santa Barbara, Calif.: Peregrine Smith, 1973.

Acknowledgements

THE original version of this study, about one-third its present length, appeared in the June 1970 issue of the *Baker Street Journal*. It was cited in several Jack London publications and, in 1974, listed in Ronald B. De Waal's *The World Bibliography of Sherlock Holmes and Dr. Watson.*

In 1974, my old friend Alvin S. Fick of Amsterdam, New York, writer and printer, suggested he bring the study out in a small, limited edition monograph. Slightly expanded and revised from its BSJ form, this book was titled *Jack London, Sherlock Holmes & Sir Arthur Conan Doyle* and was beautifully designed and printed by Mr. Fick. It was reviewed, to my surprise, in such journals as *American Literary Realism, Abstracts of English Studies,* and the *Jack London Newsletter,* among others, and is now a collector's item.

In the ten years since I sent the original article to Julian Wolff of the BSJ, I have collected a file of notes on the subject of the Jack London-Conan Doyle kinship. A good part of this material has come to me as suggestions from others who have given the matter some thought, principally the growing legion of Jack London devotees and scholars. To my knowledge, I am still the only person to have written on this subject, but certainly not the only one who knows something about it.

The opportunity to expand this work came about through a suggestion made to Jack Tracy of Gaslight Publications by John Bennett Shaw, B.S.I. of Santa Fe, New Mexico, investitured member of the Baker Street Irregulars and a long-time friend.

I do not claim, as has been said of Holmes's monograph on the polyphonic motets of Lassus, that this book represents the last word on the subject. But it might be close to that.

I should like to express my great appreciation to a number of people who have helped me throughout the ten-year development of this study: Dr. Julian Wolff, Commissionaire of the B.S.I.

and editor emeritus of the *Baker Street Journal*; Judge S. Tupper Bigelow of Toronto, who searched his cardfile for me in 1969 and said I had found a rare piece of untrammeled critical ground; the late Prof. H. W. Starr, who read my original article in manuscript and offered some priceless guidance; Russ Kingman, Jack London biographer and authority, for a valuable critique; and such other London scholars as Dr. Hensley Woodbridge of Carbondale, Ill., Dennis Hensley of Muncie, Ind., Sal Noto of Cupertino, Calif., Earle Labor of Shreveport, La., and Richard Weiderman of Cedar Springs, Mich., for help in various ways over the years.

My greatest debt in this new and greatly expanded study is to Howard Lachtman of Stockton, Calif., among the most distinguished Jack London scholars in America and also a long-time student of the Sherlock Holmes adventures. I sought his advice from the outset and have benefited greatly from what he freely gave me.

Dale L. Walker is the author of eight published books, including biographies of American radical journalist John Reed and William O. "Buckey" O'Neill, a hero of Roosevelt's Rough Riders. In twenty-five years of freelancing, he has also published about 400 magazine articles, with an emphasis on nineteenth-century American history, military history, and the American West. His most recent book is *Only the Clouds Remain,* the story of Rear Admiral Edwin C. Parsons of the Lafayette Escadrille, published by Alandale Press.

Walker is books editor for the El Paso *Times,* editor of the Western Writers of America's monthly magazine *Roundup,* News Director at the University of Texas at El Paso since 1966, a former newspaperman and television reporter. His short-story series about a police reporter named Bailey appears in *Ellery Queen's* and *Alfred Hitchcock's* mystery magazines.

Walker is married and lives in El Paso with his wife and five children.

Among his published works are a prolific number about Jack London—nearly fifty magazine and journal articles and reviews, two anthologies, and a book-length bibliography of London's fiction. Walker's interest in London dates to the mid-1940s, and when he was stationed in Alaska with the U.S. Navy in 1958-59, he traveled over some of London's Klondike country.